1

ANGER

"He that is slow to anger is better than the mighty; and he that ruleth his spirit than he that taketh a city."

–Proverbs 16:32
The Holy Bible

"Anger Is Simply Passion Requiring An Appropriate Focus."

-MIKE MURDOCK

- 1 -

2

APPEARANCE

"Strength and honour are her clothing; and she shall rejoice in time to come."

-Proverbs 31:25
The Holy Bible

"People See What You Are Before They Hear What You Are."
-MIKE MURDOCK

3

ASSIGNMENT

"Before I formed thee in the belly I knew thee; and before thou camest forth out of the womb I sanctified thee, and I ordained thee a prophet unto the nations."

–Jeremiah 1:5
The Holy Bible

"Those Who Unlock Your Compassion Are Those To Whom You Are Assigned."
-MIKE MURDOCK

CHILDREN

"Lo, children are an heritage of the Lord: and the fruit of the womb is his reward. As arrows are in the hand of a mighty man; so are children of the youth."

–Psalm 127:3,4
The Holy Bible

"The Proof Of Love
Is The Investment Of Time."
-MIKE MURDOCK

CHURCH

"One thing have I desired of the Lord, that will I seek after; that I may dwell in the house of the Lord all the days of my life, to behold the beauty of the Lord, and to enquire in His temple. For in the time of trouble He shall hide me in His pavilion: in the secret of His tabernacle shall He hide me; He shall set me up upon a rock."

–Psalm 27:4,5
The Holy Bible

"Where You Are Determines What Grows In You...Your Strength Or Your Weakness."
-MIKE MURDOCK

6

CIRCLE OF COUNSEL

"Where no counsel is, the people fall: but in the multitude of counsellors there is safety."

–Proverbs 11:14
The Holy Bible

"The Proof Of Humility
Is The Willingness To Reach."
-MIKE MURDOCK

CRITICAL ATTITUDE

"Death and life are in the power of the tongue: and they that love it shall eat the fruit thereof."

–Proverbs 18:21
The Holy Bible

"Your Words Reveal
Your Focus."

-MIKE MURDOCK

8

DEBT

"But my God shall supply all your need according to His riches in glory by Christ Jesus."

–Philippians 4:19
The Holy Bible

"The Proof Of Wisdom Is The Willingness To Wait."
-MIKE MURDOCK

DISCIPLINE

"Correct thy son, and he shall give thee rest; yea, he shall give delight unto thy soul."

–Proverbs 29:17
The Holy Bible

"Conduct Permitted Is Conduct Taught."

-MIKE MURDOCK

10

FAITH

"For verily I say unto you, That whosoever shall say unto this mountain, Be thou removed, and be thou cast into the sea; and shall not doubt in his heart, but shall believe that those things which he saith shall come to pass; he shall have whatsoever he saith. Therefore I say unto you, What things soever ye desire, when ye pray, believe that ye receive them, and ye shall have them."

–Mark 11:23,24
The Holy Bible

"God's Only Pain Is To Be Doubted...
His Only Pleasure Is To Be Believed."
-MIKE MURDOCK

11

FINANCE

"Beloved, I wish above all things that thou mayest prosper and be in health, even as thy soul prospereth."

–3 John 1:2
The Holy Bible

"Prosperity Is Simply Having Enough Of God's Provision To Complete Your Assignment."
-MIKE MURDOCK

12

FOCUS

"Brethren, I count not myself to have apprehended: but this one thing I do, forgetting those things which are behind, and reaching forth unto those things which are before, I press toward the mark for the prize of the high calling of God in Christ Jesus."

–Philippians 3:13,14
The Holy Bible

"The Only Reason Men Fail Is Broken Focus."

-MIKE MURDOCK

13

FORGIVENESS

For if ye forgive men their trespasses, your heavenly Father will also forgive you: But if ye forgive not men their trespasses, neither will your Father forgive your trespasses."

–Matthew 6:14,15
The Holy Bible

"What You Make Happen For Others, God Will Make Happen For You."
-MIKE MURDOCK

14

GENTLENESS

"And the servant of the Lord must not strive; but be gentle unto all men, apt to teach, patient,"

-2 Timothy 2:24
The Holy Bible

"The Kindest Word Is An Unkind Word Unsaid."
-MIKE MURDOCK

15

GOSSIP

"Whoso keepeth his mouth and his tongue keepeth his soul from troubles."

–Proverbs 21:23
The Holy Bible

"Silence Cannot Be Misquoted."
-MIKE MURDOCK

16

HEALTH

"And said, If thou wilt diligently hearken to the voice of the Lord thy God, and wilt do that which is right in His sight, and wilt give ear to His commandments, and keep all His statutes, I will put none of these diseases upon thee, which I have brought upon the Egyptians: for I am the Lord that healeth thee.

–Exodus 15:26
The Holy Bible

"You Have No Right To Anything You Have Not Pursued."
-MIKE MURDOCK

17

LISTENING

"Wherefore, my beloved brethren, let every man be swift to hear, slow to speak, slow to wrath:"

–James 1:19
The Holy Bible

"The Proof Of Love
Is The Willingness To Listen."
-MIKE MURDOCK

18

MISTAKES

"For a just man falleth seven times, and riseth up again: but the wicked shall fall into mischief."

–Proverbs 24:16
The Holy Bible

"All Men Fall
The Great Ones Get Back Up."
-MIKE MURDOCK

19

PAIN

"...weeping may endure for a night, but joy cometh in the morning."
-Psalm 30:5
The Holy Bible

"Nothing Is Ever As Bad As It First Appears."
-MIKE MURDOCK

20

PATIENCE

"And let us not be weary in well doing: for in due season we shall reap, if we faint not."
-Galatians 6:9
The Holy Bible

"The Proof Of Love Is The Investment Of Time."
-MIKE MURDOCK

21

PEACE

"And the peace of God, which passeth all understanding, shall keep your hearts and minds through Christ Jesus."

–Philippians 4:7
The Holy Bible

"Your Focus Is Deciding Your Present Feelings."
-MIKE MURDOCK

22

PRAYER

"If ye abide in Me, and My words abide in you, ye shall ask what ye will, and it shall be done unto you."

–John 15:7
The Holy Bible

"You Have No Right To Anything You Have Not Pursued."

-MIKE MURDOCK

23

PRIORITIES

"But seek ye first the kingdom of God, and His right-eousness; and all these things shall be added unto you."

–Matthew 6:33
The Holy Bible

"What You Do First Determines What God Does Second."

-MIKE MURDOCK

24

RELATIONSHIPS

"He that walketh with wise men shall be wise: but a companion of fools shall be destroyed."

–Proverbs 13:20
The Holy Bible

"Every Relationship In Your Life Is A Current Moving You Toward Your Dreams Or Away From Them."

-MIKE MURDOCK

25

REST

"In God have I put my trust: I will not be afraid what man can do unto me."

–Psalm 56:11
The Holy Bible

"Your Future Is Being Decided By The Person You Have Chosen To Trust."
-MIKE MURDOCK

26

SEED-FAITH

"Give, and it shall be given unto you; good measure, pressed down, and shaken together, and running over, shall men give into your bosom. For with the same measure that ye mete withal it shall be measured to you again."

–Luke 6:38
The Holy Bible

"Something God Has Given You Will Create Anything Else God Has Promised You."
-MIKE MURDOCK

27

SPIRITUAL WARFARE

"For we wrestle not against flesh and blood, but against principalities, against powers, against the rulers of the darkness of this world, against spiritual wickedness in high places."

–Ephesians 6:12
The Holy Bible

"Warfare Always Surrounds The Birth Of A Miracle."
-MIKE MURDOCK

28

STRENGTH

"But they that wait upon the Lord shall renew their strength; they shall mount up with wings as eagles; they shall run, and not be weary; and they shall walk, and not faint."

–Isaiah 40:31
The Holy Bible

"The Presence Of God Is The Only Place Your Weakness Will Die."
-MIKE MURDOCK

29

THE SECRET PLACE

"He that dwelleth in The Secret Place of the most High shall abide under the shadow of the Almighty."

–Psalm 91:1
The Holy Bible

"The Holy Spirit Is The Only Person Capable Of Being Contented With You."
-MIKE MURDOCK

30

WISDOM

"Wisdom is the principal thing; therefore get wisdom: and with all thy getting get understanding."

–Proverbs 4:7
The Holy Bible

"Ignorance Is the Only Weapon Your Enemy Can Effectively Use Against You."
-MIKE MURDOCK

31

WORD OF GOD

"Great peace have they which love thy law: and nothing shall offend them."

–Psalm 119:165
The Holy Bible

"What Enters You Determines
What Exits You."
-MIKE MURDOCK

DECISION

Will You Accept Jesus As Your Personal Savior Today?

The Bible says, "That if thou shalt confess with thy mouth the Lord Jesus, and shalt believe in thine heart that God hath raised Him from the dead, thou shalt be saved" (Romans 10:9).

Pray this prayer from your heart today! *"Dear Jesus, I believe that You died for me and rose again on the third day. I confess I am a sinner...I need Your love and forgiveness...Come into my heart. Forgive my sins. I receive Your eternal life. Confirm Your love by giving me peace, joy and supernatural love for others. Amen."*

☐ Yes, Mike! I made a decision to accept Christ as my personal Savior today. Please send me my free gift of your book *"31 Keys to a New Beginning"* to help me with my new life in Christ. *(B-48)*

NAME _____

ADDRESS _____

CITY _____ STATE _____ ZIP _____

PHONE ( ) _____ EMAIL _____

Mail To: **The Wisdom Center** *(B-174)*
P.O. Box 99 · Denton, TX 76202
1-888-WISDOM-1 (1-888-947-3661)
Website: www.thewisdomcenter.tv

Unless otherwise indicated, all Scripture quotations are taken from the King James Version of the Bible.
31 Scriptures Every Mother Should Memorize · ISBN 1-56394-268-2/B-174
Copyright © 2003 by **MIKE MURDOCK**
All publishing rights belong exclusively to Wisdom International
Published by The Wisdom Center · P.O. Box 99 · Denton, Texas 76202
1-888-WISDOM-1 (1-888-947-3661) · Website: www.thewisdomcenter.tv
Printed in the United States of America. All rights reserved under International Copyright Law. Contents and/or cover may not be reproduced in whole or in part in any form without the expressed written consent of the publisher.
0403/025k

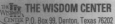

NO POSTAGE
NECESSARY
IF MAILED
IN THE
UNITED STATES

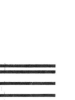

BUSINESS REPLY MAIL
FIRST CLASS   PERMIT NO. 4459   DENTON, TEXAS

POSTAGE WILL BE PAID BY ADDRESSEE

MIKE MURDOCK

P.O. BOX 99

Denton, TX 76202-9951

Your Search Is Over.

- **17 Facts You Should Know About The Holy Spirit…p. 13-17**
- **The Greatest Weapon The Holy Spirit Has Given You…p. 17**
- **15 Facts About Love… p. 28-31**
- **17 Facts Every Christian Should Know About Grieving The Holy Spirit…p. 32-37**
- **17 Facts You Should Know About The Anointing…p. 60**
- **3 Ways The Holy Spirit Will Talk To You…p. 95-100**
- **8 Important Facts About Your Assignment… p. 83-84**
- **And much more!**

The Holy Spirit, The Assignment, and The Seed.
These three vital topics deserve your Total Focus:
The Holy Spirit Is The *Source* Of Your Life.
The Assignment Is The *Reason* For Your Life.
The Seed Is The *Provision* For Your Life.

B-174

Order from our website: www.thewisdomcenter.tv

Wisdom Is The Principal Thing
The Wisdom Center
$10
B-101

THE 3
MIKE MURDOCK
Over 3 Million Mike Murdock Books In Print
MOST IMPORTANT THINGS IN YOUR LIFE

Order Today!
1-888-WISDOM-1
(1-888-947-3661)

The Wisdom Center
P.O. Box 99
Denton, Texas 76202
www.thewisdomcenter.tv

THE WISDOM CENTER

1-888-WISDOM-1 (1-888-947-3661)

Mon.-Fri.
8 AM-5 PM CST

visit us at:
www.thewisdomcenter.tv

PRODUCT NUMBER	PRODUCT DESCRIPTION	QTY	PRICE	TOTAL

Name

Address

City _____ State _____ Zip _____

Phone _____ Email _____

Method of Payment
☐ Cash ☐ Check ☐ Visa ☐ MC ☐ Amex ☐ Discover

Card# _____

Birthday _____ MO _____ DAY

Expiration Date _____

Signature _____

Total Enclosed $ _____

(Sorry No C.O.D.'s)

SubTotal	$
Canada ADD 20%	$
S/H Add 10%	$
TOTAL	$
My Seed Offering	$

Your Seed Faith Offering is used to support the MIKE MURDOCK Evangelistic Association, The Wisdom Center, and all its programs. Applicable law requires that we have the discretion to allocate donations in order to carry out our charitable purpose. In the event MMEA receives more funds for the project than needed, excess will be used for another worthy outreach.

B-174

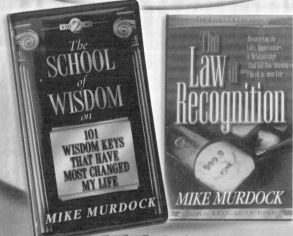

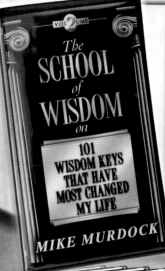

UNCOMMON WISDOM FOR UNCOMMON POWER

THE Power 7

The Power 7 Pak

► Seeds of Wisdom on The Secret Place (B-115 / $5)
► Seeds of Wisdom on The Holy Spirit (B-116 / $5)
► Seeds of Wisdom on Your Assignment (B-122 / $5)
► Seeds of Wisdom on Goal Setting (B-127 / $5)
► My Personal Dream Book (B-143 / $5)
► 101 Wisdom Keys (B-45 / $5)
► 31 Keys To A New Beginning (B-48 / $5)

The Wisdom Center
All 7 Books Only $20
WBL-19
Wisdom Is The Principal Thing

Add 10% For S/H

—

  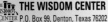

Financial Success.

- 8 Scriptural Reasons You Should Pursue Financial Prosperity

- The Secret Prayer Key You Need When Making A Financial Request To God

- The Weapon Of Expectation And The 5 Miracles It Unlocks

- How To Discern Those Who Qualify To Receive Your Financial Assistance

- How To Predict The Miracle Moment God Will Schedule Your Financial Breakthrough

- Habits Of Uncommon Achievers

- The Greatest Success Law I Ever Discovered

- How To Discern Your Place Of Assignment, The Only Place Financial Provision Is Guaranteed

- 3 Secret Keys In Solving Problems For Others

The Uncommon Woman

▸ **Master Keys In Understanding The Man In Your Life**

▸ **The One Thing Every Man Attempts To Move Away From**

▸ **The Dominant Difference Between A Wrong Woman And A Right Woman**

▸ **What Causes Men To Withdraw**

MIKE MURDOCK

THE WISDOM FOR WOMEN SERIES

THIRTY-ONE SECRETS of an UNFORGETTABLE WOMAN

Master Secrets from the life of Ruth

THE PROVERBS 31 Woman

MIKE MURDOCK

THE MENTORSHIP PROGRAM OF WISDOM

THE WISDOM CENTER
MIKE MURDOCK • P.O. Box 99 • Denton, Texas

31 Secrets of an Unforgettable Woman

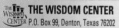

THE WISDOM CENTER
P.O. Box 99, Denton, Texas 76202

1-888-WISDOM1
(1-888-947-3661)

Website:
WWW.THEWISDOMCENTER.TV

E

UNCOMMON WISDOM FOR AN UNCOMMON MINISTRY

FOR *Ministers* ONLY

Volume 1	B-
Volume 2	B-
Volume 3	B-
Volume 4	B-
Volume 5	B-
Volume 6	B-
Volume 7	B-

When God wants to touch a nation, He raises up a preacher. It is Uncommon Men and Women of God who have driven back the darkness and shielded the unlearned and rebellious from devastation by satanic forces. They offer the breath of life to a dead world. They open Golden Doors to Change. They unleash Forces of Truth in an age of deception.

An Uncommon Minister is prepared through seasons of pain, encounters with God, a mentors. Having sat at the feet of Uncommon Mentors his entire life, Dr. Mike Murdock shar practical but personal keys to increase the excellence and productivity of your ministry. Ea volume of "The Uncommon Minister" is handy, convenient and easy to read. Your load will lighter, your journey happier, and your effectiveness increased in "doing the will of the Father

F  **THE WISDOM CENTER**
P.O. Box 99, Denton, Texas 76202

1-888-WISDOM1
(1-888-947-3661)

Website:
WWW.THEWISDOMCENTER.TV

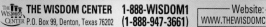

My Gift Of Appreciation...

The Wisdom Commentary

The Wisdom Commentary includes
52 topics...for mentoring your
family every week of the year.

These topics include:

- Abilities
- Achievement
- Anointing
- Assignment
- Bitterness
- Blessing
- Career
- Change
- Children
- Dating
- Depression
- Discipline
- Divorce
- Dreams And Goals
- Enemy
- Enthusiasm
- Favor
- Finances
- Fools

- Giving
- Goal-Setting
- God
- Happiness
- Holy Spirit
- Ideas
- Intercession
- Jobs
- Loneliness
- Love
- Mentorship
- Ministers
- Miracles
- Mistakes
- Money
- Negotiation
- Prayer
- Problem-Solving
- Prot g s

- Satan
- Secret Place
- Seed-Faith
- Self-Confidence
- Struggle
- Success
- Time-Management
- Understanding
- Victory
- Weaknesses
- Wisdom
- Word Of God
- Words
- Work

Gift Of Appreciation
For Your
Sponsorship
Seed of $100
or More
Gift Of Appreciation

My Gift Of Appreciation To My Sponsors!
...Those Who Sponsor One Square Foot In
The Completion Of The Wisdom Center!

Thank you so much for becoming a part of this wonderful project...The completion of The Wisdom Center.
The total purchase and renovation cost of this facility (10,000 square feet) is just over $1,000,000. This
approximately $100 per square foot. **The Wisdom Commentary is my Gift of Appreciation for you**
Sponsorship Seed of $100...that sponsors one square foot of The Wisdom Center. Become a Sponsor! Yo
will love this Volume 1, of The Wisdom Commentary. It is my exclusive Gift of Appreciation for The Wisdo
Key Family who partners with me in the Work of God as a Sponsor.   Add 10% For S/H

H **THE WISDOM CENTER**   **1-888-WISDOM1**   Website:
P.O. Box 99, Denton, Texas 76202   **(1-888-947-3661)**   WWW.THEWISDOMCENTER.TV